The NatureTrail Book of
GARDEN WILD

Su Swallow

First published in 1980 by
Usborne Publishing Ltd
Usborne House
83-85 Saffron Hill
London EC1N 8RT, England.

Written by
Su Swallow

Edited by
Bridget Gibbs and Helen Gilks

Consultant editors
Michael Chinery and
Denis Owen

Additional advice from
Alfred Leutscher

Designed by
Sally Burrough and Niki Overy

Illustrated by
John Barber, Joyce Bee,
Michelle Emblem, John Francis,
David Hurrell, Jonathan Langley,
Robert Morton, David Palmer,
Julie Piper, Barry Raynor

Printed in Belgium

The NatureTrail Book of
GARDEN WILDLIFE

About this book

This book is about the many kinds of animals and plants that live and grow in gardens. Any garden, however small, is a fascinating place to explore. You have only to turn over a stone, disturb a small area of soil, or move a pile of dead leaves to find a world of activity.

This book tells you how and where to look for wildlife in gardens. It shows you how many of the animals and plants live, and how to collect and study them. Most important of all, the book shows how you can help to protect wildlife, by providing food and shelter which will encourage animals and plants to live in your garden.

Contents

Wildlife in your garden

Gardens are very important for wildlife. Even in a backyard with a few flower pots and a hedge or wall, there can be exciting discoveries to be made. The kinds of animals and wild flowers that you find in your garden will depend partly on where you live (see page 28), how old the garden is, and the food and shelter it offers.

Most of the animals that share your garden with you are useful. By watching them and understanding how they all live together, you will be able to enjoy your garden all the more.

Each part of the garden, from the flower beds to the compost heap, is a separate habitat with its own inhabitants and visitors. This picture shows some of the places to explore and what to look for in them.

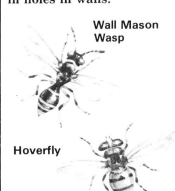

You will not find many animals in a new garden like this one because there is no food or shelter for them. You can help attract wildlife straightaway, by making a bird table (see page 9) and a pond (see page 24). More animals will come as plants begin to grow.

Insects, such as hoverflies, rest on walls, especially in sunny spots. The Wall Mason Wasp builds its nest in holes in walls.

Wall Mason Wasp

Hoverfly

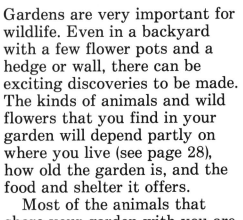

Great Spotted Woodpecker

Cardinal Beetle

Eyed Hawk Moth

Many animals live in a tree. Look for birds and insects, such as beetles and moths.

Smooth Newt

A pond will attract frogs, newts and insects, such as dragonflies.

Common Frog

Shrubs hide birds' nests and insects, like the Speckled Bush-cricket. Hedgehogs may hibernate in leaves under hedges.

Speckled Bush-cricket

Hedgehog

Many small animals live among the rotting plants of compost heaps. Look for worms, millipedes, centipedes, beetles and harvestmen.

Centipede

Brandling Earthworm

In winter, look in corners of garden sheds for spiders and hibernating ladybirds. Wood mice may build nests in sheds.

Two-spot Ladybird

House Spider

Wood Mouse

Look under logs and stones, and in other damp, dark places for animals like woodlice.

Woodlouse

Bees and butterflies visit flowers to feed on nectar.

Bumble Bee

Orange-tip Butterfly

Flower borders provide cover for snails, caterpillars and slugs.

Dot Moth caterpillar

Brown-lipped Snail

Blackbird

5

Life in the soil

The soil in your garden is full of small animals, although many are too tiny to see. Different kinds of animals and plants need different types of soil. Snails, for instance, need lime in the soil for making their shells. Moles will visit your garden only if the soil is soft enough for them to dig in.

You should be able to find several of these garden animals by digging in the soil. Some, like the earthworm, help to keep the soil healthy, but a few damage plants by feeding on the roots.

Worms

If one end of a worm is cut off, the remaining part can usually grow to form a complete worm again.

Worms cannot live above ground. If dug up, they burrow immediately back into the ground.

A worm can grip tightly to the sides of its burrow with the tiny bristles on its body. This makes it difficult for birds to pull worms out of the ground.

Some worms deposit their waste soil or "casts" above ground.

Some worms emerge at night to look for leaves. They pull them down into their burrows for food.

Waste soil

Nibbled leaves decay and enrich the soil.

This band is involved with egg-laying. It is not a scar.

Some kinds of worms rest in summer.

Worm tunnels allow air and water to move around plant roots

Huge numbers of worms live in the ground, especially under lawns where the soil is not disturbed. Worms swallow soil and feed on the rotting plant and animal matter it contains.

They then pass the soil out of their bodies, usually just below the ground surface. This soil often contains minerals from deeper in the ground which are valuable to plants.

Underground slugs

Shelled Slug

Most slugs live above the ground and feed on plants. Shelled Slugs live underground and feed on earthworms. On warm damp nights they also come above the ground to feed.

Animals that come out of the ground

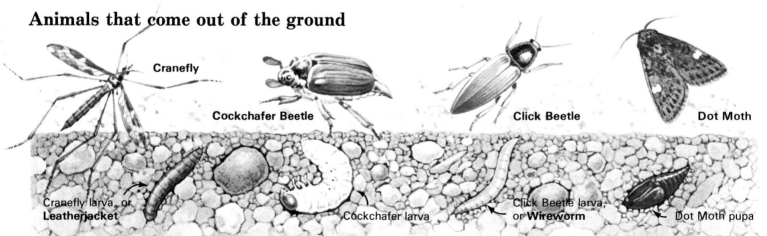

Cranefly

Cockchafer Beetle

Click Beetle

Dot Moth

Cranefly larva, or **Leatherjacket**

Cockchafer larva

Click Beetle larva, or **Wireworm**

Dot Moth pupa

Several insects found in gardens start life in the soil. For example, some beetles and flies lay their eggs in soil. When the young insects or "larvae" hatch, they feed on plant roots. It may be several years before the adult insects emerge above ground. Some moth caterpillars form pupae (see page 14) in the soil. If you dig up a pupa, try keeping it in a cool place until the adult moth emerges. Put the pupa on sand in a box with a few twigs.

Making a wormery

Leaves for worms to feed on

Brown paper and string

Put alternate layers of fine sand and soil in a large glass jar. Then put in a few worms from the garden and some leaves for them to feed on. Wrap paper round the jar to keep the light out. Remove the paper a day or two later and you will see how the worms have mixed up the layers of sand and soil.

Looking at soil

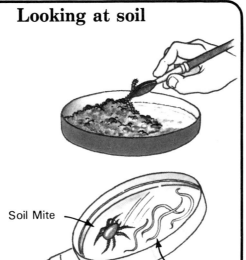

Soil Mite

Round Worms

There are millions of minute animals in the top layer of a square metre of soil. Try to find some of them by putting some soil in a dish with a little water. Pick up the tiny creatures on a paint brush and use a magnifying glass to examine them more closely.

Food webs

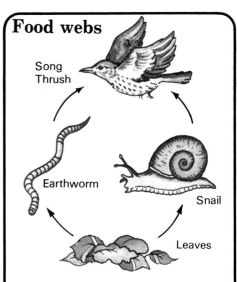

Song Thrush

Earthworm

Snail

Leaves

All animals depend on one another and on plants for food. This picture shows how the earthworm and snail feed on leaves and they in turn are eaten by thrushes. Eating patterns like this are called "food webs". Most animals eat a variety of food, so food webs are usually more complicated than this.

Moles

Mole fur lies easily in any direction and does not ruffle. This allows the mole to move backwards down its tunnels without difficulty.

Nest of dead leaves, grass and moss.

Strong legs and large feet for pushing soil away.

Larder of worms

Many kinds of animals eat worms. Moles probably eat at least fifty a day. They also store worms in an underground larder. The mole bites off the worm's head end to stop it escaping, but if the worm is not eaten it grows a new head end and can escape. Moles spend most of their time underground. Mounds and ridges of earth show where they have been tunnelling. When they do come to the surface it is usually during the breeding season or to hunt for food on a damp night.

7

How to attract wildlife

A neat, tidy garden with no overgrown patches offers little shelter to wildlife. A small corner of long grass and nettles, where dead plants are left to decay instead of being cleared away, is sufficient to attract many insects. These in turn encourage visits from larger animals that prey on them.

You could provide a few artificial habitats where animals can hide, build their nests or hibernate. You could also grow some of the plants shown here and on page 15 which provide food for insects and birds.

Some climbing plants offer food and shelter to animals. Birds may build their nests in them in spring, and feed on any berries in winter. The Holly Blue survives the winter as a pupa (see page 14) amongst Ivy leaves.

Holly Blue Butterfly

Song Thrush

Cotoneaster

Ivy

Magpie

Some bees and wasps live alone in small holes, like those in a ventilation brick. You could put one in your garden.

Mournful Wasp

Solitary Bee

Wedge a flower pot or an old jug in a hedge or bank to provide a nesting site for birds. Put some dried grass in it.

Wren

Dead leaves under a hedge or shrub might encourage a **Hedgehog** to hibernate there.

Leave fallen fruit for butterflies and wasps to feed on.

A piece of corrugated iron or a plank of wood on rough grass could shelter a toad, Slow Worms, beetles or a Field Mouse's nest.

Devil's Coach Horse Beetle

Common Toad

If you leave a fallen log or branch on the ground, fungi and mosses will grow on it, while beetles and other small animals will live in the decaying wood.

Peacock Butterfly

Some flowers, like **Michaelmas Daisies**, attract butterflies to feed on their nectar.

Feeding birds

Bird table

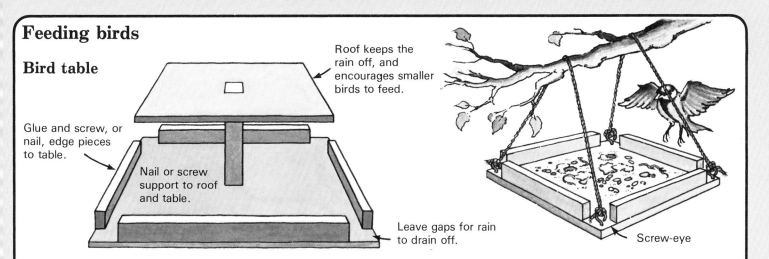

Roof keeps the rain off, and encourages smaller birds to feed.

Glue and screw, or nail, edge pieces to table.

Nail or screw support to roof and table.

Leave gaps for rain to drain off.

Screw-eye

Many kinds of birds will visit your garden to feed from a bird table, especially in winter. To make this simple bird table, use a piece of plywood for the base and thin strips of wood for the edges. To make a roof for the table, use another piece of plywood and a thick strip of wood to support it. Fix the table to a post or hang it from a tree. Remember to wash it regularly.

To hang your table from a tree, fix a screw-eye at each corner and make two loops with thick string. When you put food out on the table, put some on the ground as well, for ground-feeding birds.

Food

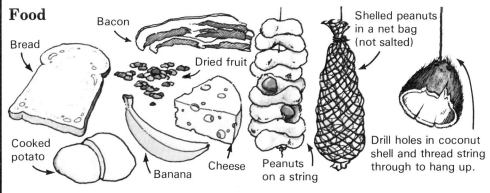

Bacon

Bread

Dried fruit

Shelled peanuts in a net bag (not salted)

Cooked potato

Banana

Cheese

Peanuts on a string

Drill holes in coconut shell and thread string through to hang up.

These are some foods that birds like. You could also collect seeds for the winter. Try thistles, groundsel and other wild plants, together with berries like hips and haws, and nuts like acorns. You can make a bird pudding by mixing kitchen scraps and uncooked porridge oats with melted fat. Put the mixture in an empty coconut shell. Use plasticine to fill the holes while the fat sets, then hang the shell upside down.

Water

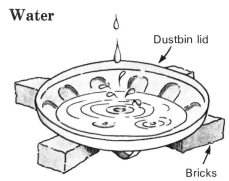

Dustbin lid

Bricks

Birds need water for drinking and bathing all through the year. Use an old tin tray, a dustbin lid or a pie dish. Change the water daily and keep it free of ice in winter.

Nesting materials

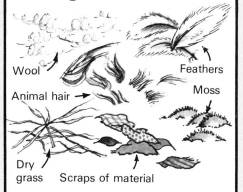

Wool

Feathers

Animal hair

Moss

Dry grass

Scraps of material

In spring, attract birds to your garden by hanging up nesting materials from a tree. You could put them in a plastic fruit net.

Dangers to wildlife

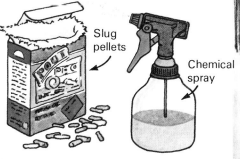

Slug pellets

Chemical spray

Pest-killers not only kill the creatures they are meant to kill, but are also likely to poison other animals that feed in the same area. Animals in the same food webs are also harmed when they eat the poisoned creatures.

Cats scare birds away and attack small mammals such as mice, voles and shrews.

Plants in the garden

For hundreds of years, fruit, vegetables and herbs were more important in gardens than flowers. They are still grown in gardens today, but many plants are also grown, not for food but for their beauty.

All garden flowers have been bred from wild plants. Some flowers are cultivated in gardens in one part of the world but still grow wild in another.

Whether gardeners want them or not, wild flowers often grow in gardens. Good places to look for them are lawns and vegetable plots.

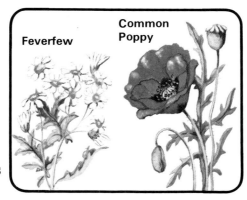

People often remove wild flowers such as these if they find them growing in their gardens, but some poppies are grown especially for their beauty, and Feverfew was once a popular garden herb used in medicine.

You are not likely to find many wild flowers growing in flower beds like this one. The bed is filled with a variety of plants of different shapes and sizes, and there is little room for seeds of wild plants to settle.

Where garden flowers come from

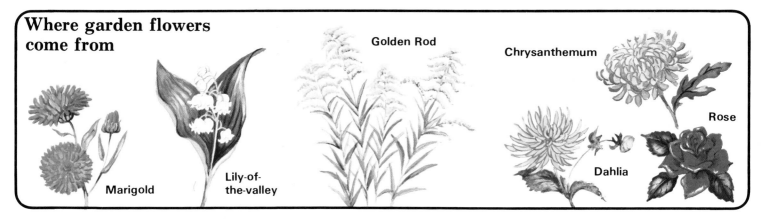

Many garden plants were once used to make medicines and cosmetics. Marigolds were used to colour cheese, and to rub on sore eyes. Lily-of-the-valley was used to make a skin tonic.

Several plants that we grow in our gardens grow wild in other countries and are thought of as weeds. Golden Rod is a common weed in North America.

Many flowers have been specially bred for the garden and look quite different from the original plants. Flowers like these three are grown for their colour and size, and attract little wildlife.

Feeding the soil

Soil needs "feeding" regularly as growing plants use up its goodness. Decaying plants enrich soil, so when you cut plants down, leave them, or put them on a compost heap to rot.

Growing wild flowers

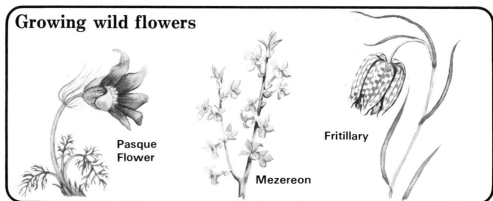

As more land is used for building and hedges are cut down and grassland ploughed up, natural habitats for wild flowers disappear. You could help to protect plants that are in danger of

dying out by growing some in your garden. If you want to do this, buy the plants from a nursery. *Never* dig up a wild plant. The wild flowers shown here are all rare in Europe.

The lawn

A lawn that is mown regularly provides the same kind of habitat for wild flowers as a field where animals graze. Some plants, like the Daisy and Plantain, survive the mowing and grazing because they grow close to the ground in rosettes. Others, like the Clover and Bird's-foot Trefoil, send out long creeping shoots. If grass is not cut down, it will grow up quickly and flower in summer.

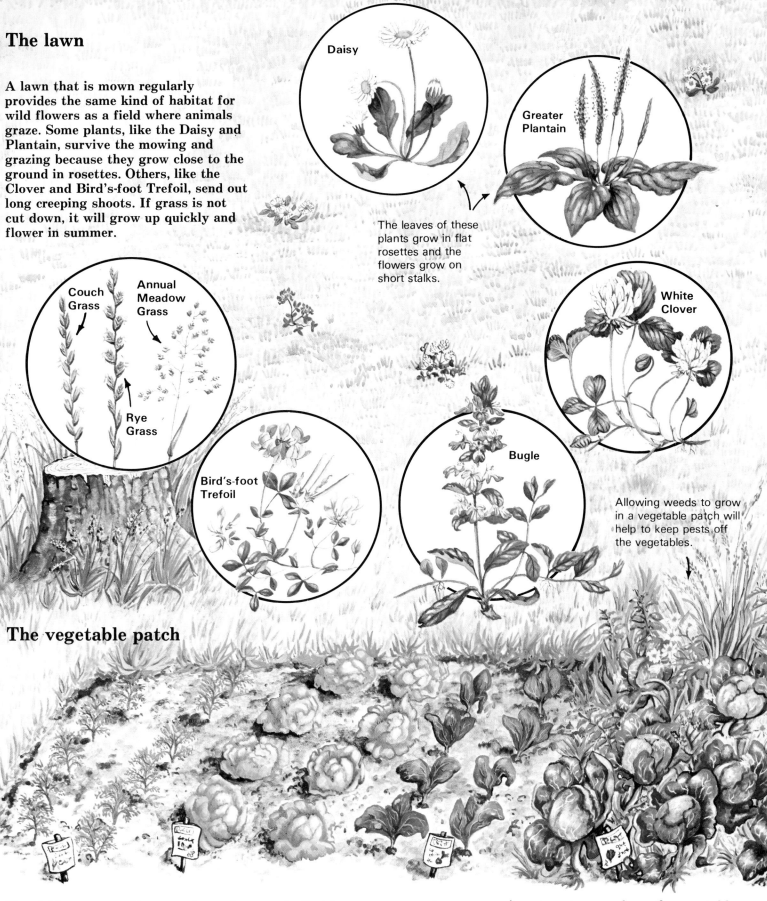

Daisy

Greater Plantain

The leaves of these plants grow in flat rosettes and the flowers grow on short stalks.

Couch Grass

Annual Meadow Grass

Rye Grass

White Clover

Bird's-foot Trefoil

Bugle

Allowing weeds to grow in a vegetable patch will help to keep pests off the vegetables.

The vegetable patch

Vegetables are usually grown in neat rows like this, so it is easy for the gardener to hoe out any wild plants that spring up uninvited. But every time the ground is hoed to remove weeds that have sprung up, large areas of bare soil are exposed where more seeds can settle and wild plants take root again. If some wild plants are allowed to grow, they help to attract insect pests away from the vegetables. They also provide cover for other insects that prey on the pests. So it is a good idea not to remove all the weeds from a vegetable patch.

More about plants

Wild flowers that invade gardens are often called weeds. The common garden weeds shown on these pages all have efficient ways of spreading and surviving. Some produce thousands of seeds, while others grow very long, tough roots. Many swamp other plants and are difficult to get rid of.

Although wild flowers are thought of as a nuisance by most gardeners, many of them are useful. They attract insects and birds, which feed on them instead of on the gardener's vegetables and showy blooms.

Weeds and seeds

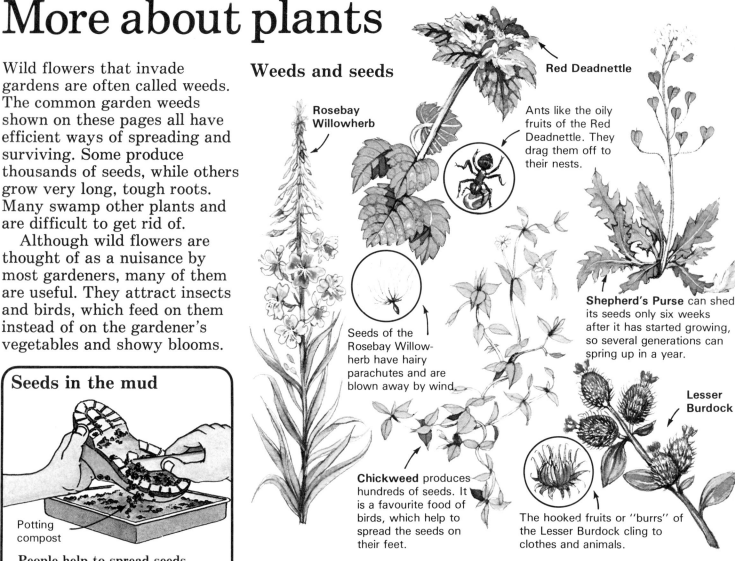

Red Deadnettle

Ants like the oily fruits of the Red Deadnettle. They drag them off to their nests.

Rosebay Willowherb

Seeds of the Rosebay Willowherb have hairy parachutes and are blown away by wind.

Shepherd's Purse can shed its seeds only six weeks after it has started growing, so several generations can spring up in a year.

Lesser Burdock

Chickweed produces hundreds of seeds. It is a favourite food of birds, which help to spread the seeds on their feet.

The hooked fruits or "burrs" of the Lesser Burdock cling to clothes and animals.

Seeds in the mud

Potting compost

People help to spread seeds, especially on their shoes and on car tyres. Try scraping the mud from shoes or a tyre on to damp potting compost and see if any weeds grow.

The success of many weeds depends both on the large number of seeds they produce and also on how efficiently the seeds are scattered away from the parent plant. Most seeds are scattered or "dispersed" either by wind or by animals and humans. Some, such as those of Rosebay Willowherb, are adaptable. In wet weather, when the hairy seeds cannot blow away in the normal way, they become sticky and get carried away on birds' bodies.

Climbing plants

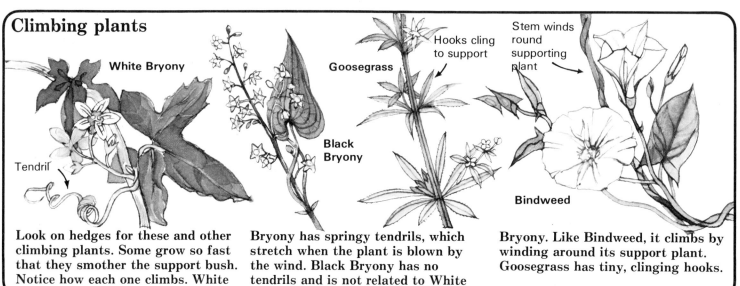

White Bryony

Tendril

Goosegrass

Hooks cling to support

Stem winds round supporting plant

Black Bryony

Bindweed

Look on hedges for these and other climbing plants. Some grow so fast that they smother the support bush. Notice how each one climbs. White

Bryony has springy tendrils, which stretch when the plant is blown by the wind. Black Bryony has no tendrils and is not related to White

Bryony. Like Bindweed, it climbs by winding around its support plant. Goosegrass has tiny, clinging hooks.

Changing shape

Dandelion

Some wild plants survive in the garden by adapting the way they grow to suit their surroundings. Plants that often grow in lawns tend to do this. In short grass, where there is plenty of light, the Dandelion grows close to the ground. Its leaves grow as a flat rosette, so it is not easily damaged by lawn mowers or trampling feet. In long grass, the Dandelion grows taller to reach the light, and has bigger, more upright leaves.

Long roots

1

Curled Dock

The main root of the Curled Dock may be as much as two metres long and is very hard to dig up. If it is broken off just below ground level, a new plant grows up from the bit of root left in the soil.

Plants without flowers

Mosses and ferns

Maidenhair Spleenwort Fern

Silky Wall Feather Moss

Old walls and shady corners of the garden are good places to look for mosses and ferns. Moss plants either grow as small dense "cushions", or they form larger creeping patches like this Silky Wall Feather Moss. Mosses and ferns do not have flowers. They produce spores instead of seeds. Moss spores develop inside tiny capsules on long stalks. Fern spores can be seen as brown patches on the underside of the fronds.

2

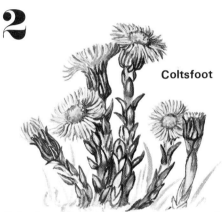

Coltsfoot

Coltsfoot has root-like underground stems which spread quickly and make it difficult to dig up. Its flowers look like Dandelions but can be recognized by their stout stems covered with pink scales.

Fungi

Grass in centre of ring grows thickly as nutrients from dead fungus threads make soil richer.

Grass around toadstools dies off as fungus threads strangle its roots.

Fairy-ring Toadstool

Purple Stereum grows on fruit trees

Fungi also produce spores. They are shed from the underside of toadstool caps. The spores germinate in the ground, giving rise to a mass of "threads" from which new toadstools can grow. The Fairy-ring Toadstool often grows in lawns. The ring gets larger every year as the underground threads reach out into fresh soil for food. Old threads inside the ring die and enrich the soil as they decay.

Some fungi grow on dead wood or living trees instead of in the ground. A few fungi are very poisonous, so never eat any you find and always wash your hands after touching them.

Butterflies and moths

Most butterflies and moths visit garden flowers in spring and summer to feed on the sugary fluid, called "nectar", which flowers produce. During winter, some hibernate but others die, having laid eggs earlier in the year. Few butterflies lay their eggs on garden plants but many moths do, so most of the caterpillars you find in gardens will belong to moths.

Moths are mainly active at night, but you may find them in the day as they rest. They are often well hidden on tree trunks, among leaves and on walls.

Butterfly or moth?

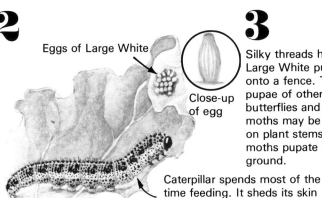

Antennae with knobs

Feathery antennae →

Moth at rest with wings closed flat.

Butterfly with wings closed up over body.

You can tell the difference between butterflies and moths by looking at their feelers or "antennae". Butterflies' antennae always have a knob at the end. Moths' antennae are usually feathery or hairlike.

Another difference is that butterflies either spread their wings out flat when they rest, or close them upright over their back; moths keep their wings closed flat, or in a tent shape over their bodies.

1 How they grow

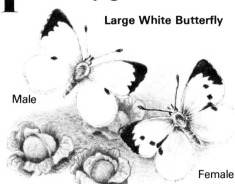

Large White Butterfly

Male

Female

A male and female butterfly often circle around each other in the air before landing to mate. Female moths generally rest on plants until a male mate arrives.

2

Eggs of Large White

Close-up of egg

Caterpillar spends most of the time feeding. It sheds its skin (moults) several times as it grows.

The female lays her eggs, singly or in clusters, on the plant which the caterpillars will feed on when they hatch. Each kind has its own particular food plants.

3

Silky threads hold the Large White pupa onto a fence. The pupae of other butterflies and some moths may be found on plant stems. Most moths pupate in the ground.

When the caterpillar is fully grown, it stops feeding and changes into a pupa. The adult butterfly or moth develops inside the pupa and hatches out in spring or summer.

Feeding

Lackey Moth caterpillars feeding on the leaves of a fruit tree inside their tent.

Small Tortoiseshell Butterfly feeding on Ice Plant

Proboscis

Close-up of mouth. Proboscis is coiled when butterfly is not feeding.

Some caterpillars spin a tent of silky thread on their food plant. They feed on the leaves inside the tent, which they make larger as they need more food.

Butterflies and moths feed on nectar which they suck from flowers with their long tube-like tongue or "proboscis". Some moths do not feed at all, as they only live a short time. They use the energy from food they ate as caterpillars.

Keeping safe

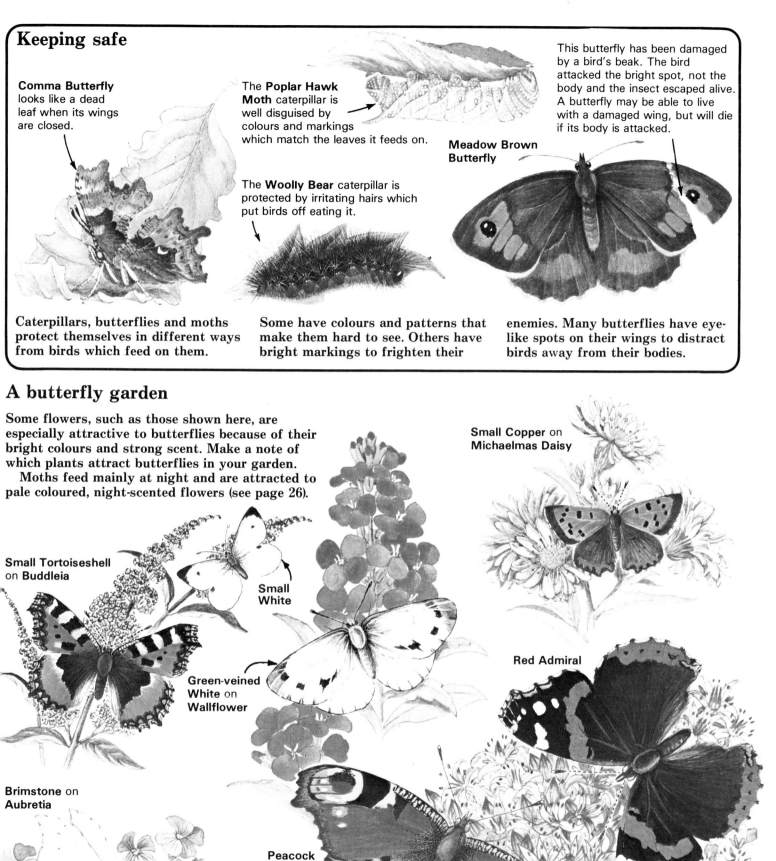

Comma Butterfly looks like a dead leaf when its wings are closed.

The **Poplar Hawk Moth** caterpillar is well disguised by colours and markings which match the leaves it feeds on.

The **Woolly Bear** caterpillar is protected by irritating hairs which put birds off eating it.

Meadow Brown Butterfly

This butterfly has been damaged by a bird's beak. The bird attacked the bright spot, not the body and the insect escaped alive. A butterfly may be able to live with a damaged wing, but will die if its body is attacked.

Caterpillars, butterflies and moths protect themselves in different ways from birds which feed on them. Some have colours and patterns that make them hard to see. Others have bright markings to frighten their enemies. Many butterflies have eye-like spots on their wings to distract birds away from their bodies.

A butterfly garden

Some flowers, such as those shown here, are especially attractive to butterflies because of their bright colours and strong scent. Make a note of which plants attract butterflies in your garden.

Moths feed mainly at night and are attracted to pale coloured, night-scented flowers (see page 26).

Small Copper on **Michaelmas Daisy**

Small Tortoiseshell on **Buddleia**

Small White

Green-veined White on **Wallflower**

Red Admiral

Brimstone on **Aubretia**

Peacock

Ice Plant

15

Garden insects

There are thousands of different insects, many of which live in gardens. All insects have six legs, and most have wings and can fly. Those that can't fly are mostly small and stay hidden. When disturbed they either keep still or scuttle out of sight.

A few insects damage garden plants, but many are useful to the gardener. Some feed on pests or dead plants or animals. Bees are important to garden plants because they carry pollen from one flower to another.

Insects and their young

1 Earwigs

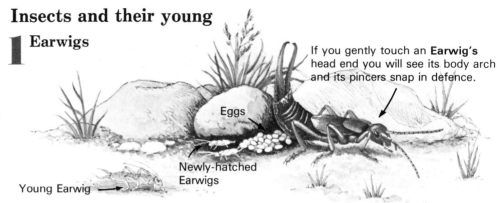

If you gently touch an **Earwig's** head end you will see its body arch and its pincers snap in defence.

Eggs

Newly-hatched Earwigs

Young Earwig

All insects go through several stages as they grow. Some, like bees, ants and butterflies (page 14), have four stages. Others, like the Earwig, have only three. The young insect grows directly into an adult and does not form a pupa. Unlike most insects, the female Earwig stays with her eggs to protect them. She also licks them to stop mould growing and feeds her young when they first hatch.

Living together

1 Ants

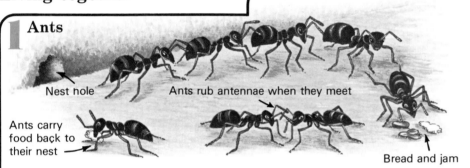

Nest hole

Ants rub antennae when they meet

Ants carry food back to their nest

Bread and jam

Most insects live alone, but ants and some bees and wasps live in colonies. Each colony has a queen, which lays eggs, winged males, and workers that look after the nest, eggs and young.

Worker ants bring male and female winged ants out of the nest for the mating flight.

In summer, the males and young queens leave the nest on a mating flight. After mating, the males die. The queens fly to the ground and make new nests underground.

You may spot a line of ants on a path moving between a nest hole and some food. The ants leave a scent trail which other ants follow. Rub your finger across the trail and see how the ants react.

Black Ant "milking" a Greenfly

Honeydew

Ants eat almost anything but especially like sweet things. Some feed on honeydew made by Greenfly. To make a Greenfly produce drops of honeydew, an ant strokes it with its antennae.

2 Bees

Bumble Bee gathering pollen

Bumble Bees live together in nests on, or under, the ground. They collect pollen from flowers and carry it back to the nest in special pollen bags on their back legs.

3 Wasps

Common Wasp carrying a caterpillar back to its nest.

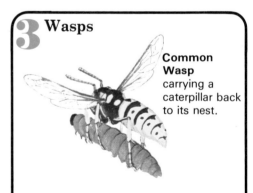

Common Wasps usually nest under the ground. The nest is made of paper, which the queen and workers make by chewing bits of wood. Wasps feed their young on insects.

2 Greenfly

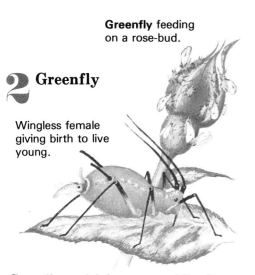

Greenfly feeding on a rose-bud.

Wingless female giving birth to live young.

Greenfly multiply very rapidly. In spring and summer, they give birth to live young and in autumn, they lay eggs. Not all Greenfly have wings, but those that do, fly to other plants to produce more young.

Insects that look alike

This **Hoverfly** looks like a bee.

Wasp Beetle looks and moves like a wasp.

Another **Hoverfly**. This one looks like a wasp.

Some insects, especially hoverflies, look like bees or wasps but have no sting. Birds learn to avoid stinging insects or anything that looks like a bee or a wasp, so the hoverflies are left alone by them. Bees and wasps have two pairs of wings, whereas hoverflies, like all flies, have only one pair.

Insects and flowers

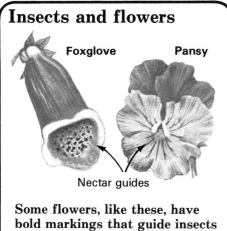

Foxglove   **Pansy**

Nectar guides

Some flowers, like these, have bold markings that guide insects to their nectar. Others appear to be plain, but have markings that only insects can see.

Clues to look for

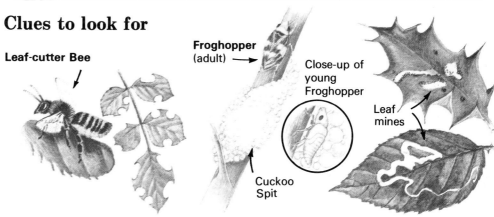

Leaf-cutter Bee

Froghopper (adult)

Close-up of young Froghopper

Leaf mines

Cuckoo Spit

Some common garden insects are not easy to find, but you can look for clues to tell you where they are. The Leaf-cutter Bee cuts pieces out of rose leaves to make tiny nests for its eggs. The young Froghopper hides in white froth, called Cuckoo Spit, which it makes as it feeds on plant juices. The larvae of some insects feed inside leaves, causing blotches or "mines" to appear on the surface of the leaves.

Trapping insects

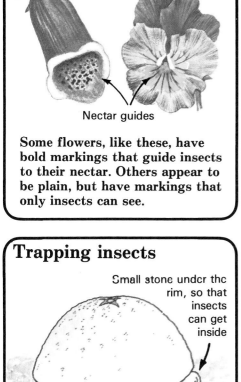

Small stone under the rim, so that insects can get inside

Place an empty grapefruit half on soil in the garden overnight. The next morning you may find woodlice and insects, such as beetles, sheltering under it. You may also find slugs and ants.

Keeping insects

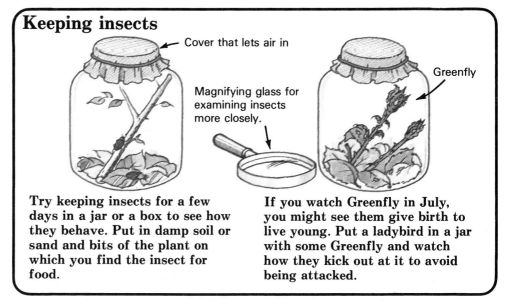

Cover that lets air in

Magnifying glass for examining insects more closely.

Greenfly

Try keeping insects for a few days in a jar or a box to see how they behave. Put in damp soil or sand and bits of the plant on which you find the insect for food.

If you watch Greenfly in July, you might see them give birth to live young. Put a ladybird in a jar with some Greenfly and watch how they kick out at it to avoid being attacked.

Snails and other small animals

All the animals on these pages are common in gardens, although they usually stay hidden among plants and under stones or bark during the day and in dry weather. This is because none of them has a waterproof skin, so they are in danger of drying out and dying. They mostly come out to feed at night or after rain.

Not all slugs and snails are harmful. If you leave a few dead plants around the garden, they will usually feed on these rather than on new crops.

Snails

Snails have long tentacles with eyes at their tips. If disturbed, the snail withdraws them.

In winter and in dry weather, snails hide away, often in cracks in walls or under stones. They retreat into their shells and seal the opening with layers of mucus that hardens as it dries.

Garden Snail

Snails leave a silvery trail of mucus.

Most snails found in the garden feed on plants. Some snails damage growing plants, but most prefer decaying leaves. They feed by filing off bits of leaf with rows of tiny teeth on their tongue.

During the day, some kinds of snail cluster together in a sheltered spot. After each feeding trip, at night or after rain, they usually return to the same place, following their own trail of slimy mucus. If you find a group of snails, mark their shells with a felt tip pen. Check each day to see if the marked snails are still there. Snails may live in the same spot for several years if undisturbed.

Lots of legs

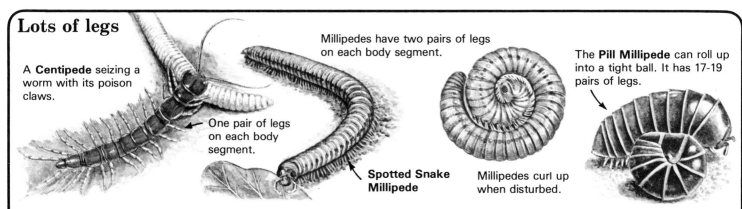

A **Centipede** seizing a worm with its poison claws.

One pair of legs on each body segment.

Millipedes have two pairs of legs on each body segment.

Spotted Snake Millipede

The **Pill Millipede** can roll up into a tight ball. It has 17-19 pairs of legs.

Millipedes curl up when disturbed.

Centipedes have one pair of legs on each segment of their bodies. They move fast and hunt insects, spiders and worms, killing them with their poison claws.

Millipedes live in the soil, under stones and bark, and in compost and leaf litter. They feed mainly on rotting plants. Most, like the Spotted Snake Millipede, look rather like centipedes, but you can tell the difference by counting the number of legs on each body segment. The Pill Millipede looks like a Woodlouse, but it has more legs.

A snail's enemy

Song Thrush

Thrush's "anvil"

In dry weather, when earthworms are scarce, Song Thrushes eat snails. They hammer the snails against a stone to break the shells. Pieces of shell are left around the stone or "anvil".

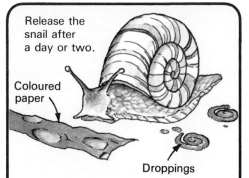

Release the snail after a day or two.

Coloured paper

Droppings

To see how snails eat, try keeping one for a couple of days and feeding it on damp coloured paper. You will soon see thin patches appear on the paper where the snail has rasped at it. The snail's droppings will be the same colour as the paper.

Slugs

Great Grey Slug

Hole for breathing

This slug has a ridge or "keel" on its body.

Slugs do not have a shell to retreat into, so in cold and dry weather they burrow deep into the soil. They protect themselves from enemies by producing an unpleasant tasting mucus.

Strawberry plant

Garden Slug

Some slugs, like this Garden Slug will feed on growing plants. To find them, put straw or rhubarb leaves around the plant. The slugs shelter there during the day, when you can remove them.

1 Mating

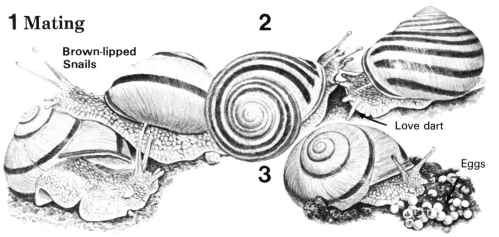

Brown-lipped Snails

2

Love dart

3

Eggs

In spring and summer you may find snails mating in the garden. During courtship, which may last several hours, the two snails crawl over each other, then fire a chalky "love dart" into each other's skin. Soon after

mating, each snail lays its round, white eggs into a hole that it makes in the ground. Three or four weeks later the eggs hatch into tiny snails, which slowly grow into adults.

Woodlice

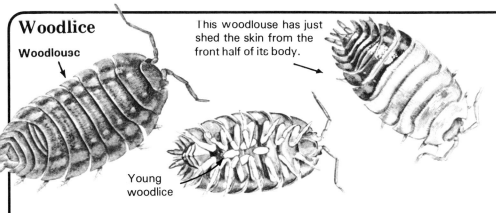

Woodlouse

This woodlouse has just shed the skin from the front half of its body.

Young woodlice

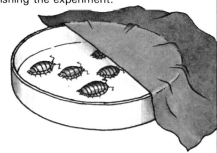

Release the woodlice after finishing the experiment.

Woodlice are common in gardens. They feed on dead plants. Female Woodlice carry their young in a pouch under their bodies. When the young hatch, they stay under their

mother's body until they are ready to live on their own. They shed their skin or "moult" several times as they grow. Woodlice have seven pairs of legs.

Woodlice like dark, damp places. If you put a few on one side of a dish and then cover the other side with a cloth, you will see that they soon move to the darkened side.

Spiders

Spiders are among the most interesting small animals in the garden. They are also very useful, as they feed on some of the insects that damage plants.

Most spiders spin webs to catch insects, but a few catch their prey without the aid of webs. All spiders kill their prey by biting it with poison fangs, and then feed by sucking the juices out of its body.

Look for spiders' webs early in the morning, especially in the autumn when dew or frost sparkles on the delicate threads and shows them up.

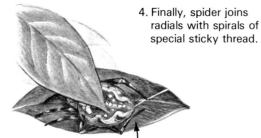

Garden Spider hiding under leaves, attached to its web by a thread.

Orb web

1. Spider makes a bridge thread from which the web will hang.

2. Threads are spun to form the framework.

4. Finally, spider joins radials with spirals of special sticky thread.

3. Spider spins "radial" threads, attached to framework and centre of web.

Spider may bind up fly in thread before eating it.

Different groups of spiders spin different kinds of webs. Some, such as the Garden Spider, build orb webs like this. The spider usually has to spin a new web each day as webs are easily destroyed by the weather. The spider may sit in its web or it may hide under leaves, joined to its web by a single thread. When an insect gets caught in the web, its struggles make the thread vibrate. The spider then comes out of hiding and attacks its prey. It often binds an insect up in silk thread before feeding on it.

Sheet web

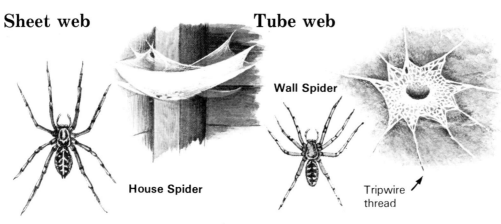

House Spider

Tube web

Wall Spider

Tripwire thread

Money Spiders

Money Spider

House Spiders spin sheet webs or "cob-webs" in corners inside sheds or houses. Their silk is not sticky, but insects get caught up in the close network of threads.

This spider often spins its tube-shaped web in cracks on walls. When an insect stumbles over one of the tripwire threads, the spider rushes out to seize it and drags it back down the tube.

Large numbers of these tiny black spiders may cover the lawn with their delicate webs. Air currents often catch the threads so that the spider is lifted up and may be carried several miles.

Watching spiders

Release the spider after a day or two.

Damp paper tissue for spider to drink from.

Cellophane

Catch a spider (a good place to look is on or near a web you find in the garden), and put it in a box with a bent coat-hanger like this. Watch the spider spin a new web, using the hanger as a support.

Spiders without webs

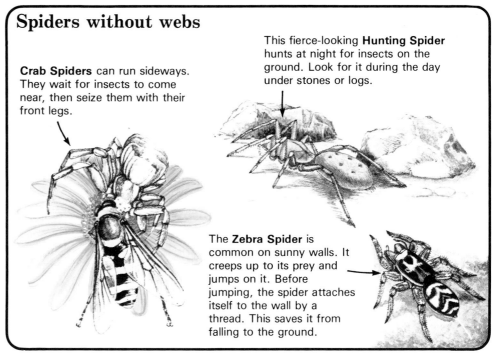

Crab Spiders can run sideways. They wait for insects to come near, then seize them with their front legs.

This fierce-looking **Hunting Spider** hunts at night for insects on the ground. Look for it during the day under stones or logs.

The **Zebra Spider** is common on sunny walls. It creeps up to its prey and jumps on it. Before jumping, the spider attaches itself to the wall by a thread. This saves it from falling to the ground.

1 How the Garden Spider breeds

Escape thread

Male

Female

Mating is a dangerous process for the male spider as there is always a chance that the female, which is larger than the male, may attack and eat him. When a male Garden Spider finds a female, he approaches her carefully, always ready to escape on a special thread that he has spun. The female may chase him away several times before mating with him. Afterwards, the male quickly escapes.

2

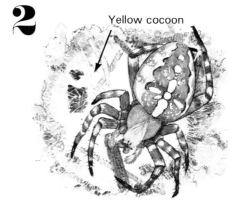

Yellow cocoon

The Garden Spider lays her eggs in autumn. She spins a cocoon of yellow thread around them, which she disguises with bits of bark and dust. Soon after, she dies. The young spiders hatch the following spring.

Wolf Spiders

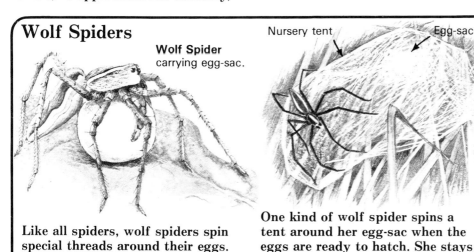

Wolf Spider carrying egg-sac.

Nursery tent

Egg-sac

Like all spiders, wolf spiders spin special threads around their eggs. Instead of hiding them in a safe place, the female carries the egg-sac with her wherever she goes.

One kind of wolf spider spins a tent around her egg-sac when the eggs are ready to hatch. She stays near it, and tears the tent open when the young spiders are ready to live on their own.

Moulting

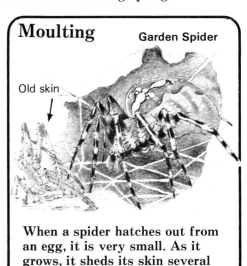

Garden Spider

Old skin

When a spider hatches out from an egg, it is very small. As it grows, it sheds its skin several times until it reaches adult size. You may find old skins on webs.

Birds

Most gardens are visited by a variety of birds all the year round. You can attract birds to your garden by putting out food and water, especially in winter, when food is scarce in the countryside. If there are trees or shrubs to provide cover, birds may even build their nests in gardens. If you find a nest, never disturb it or the parent birds may abandon it.

Watch birds quietly and make notes to help you identify them. Notice their size, shape, colour and any special markings.

Collared Dove

The **Great Tit** is larger than the Blue Tit and has a black cap.

Greenfinch

The **Green Woodpecker** visits gardens and looks for ants on the lawn.

Greenfinches and Blue Tits are common visitors to gardens when food is put out for them. (See page 9).

Blue Tits

The **Treecreeper** looks for insects in bark. It circles tree trunks, always moving upwards from the base.

The **Pied Wagtail** hunts insects on lawns. Its tail bobs up and down.

The **Chaffinch** feeds on the ground and mostly eats small seeds.

The **Bullfinch** eats seeds but also feeds on the buds of fruit trees and bushes.

The **Nuthatch** hops up and down tree trunks in search of insects to eat.

The **Goldfinch** feeds on plant seeds, but attacks Dandelion flowers in spring.

The **Blackbird** can often be seen singing from a tree top or a chimney stack.

The **Wren** is a tiny bird with a short, up-turned tail. It flies back and forth in straight lines and never keeps still for long.

The **Dunnock** feeds on insects and seeds. It stays near the cover of hedges and shrubs.

House Sparrows take dust baths in dry soil to help clean their feathers.

A male **Robin** often claims a garden as his territory. He keeps all other Robins out except for his mate.

Spot the difference

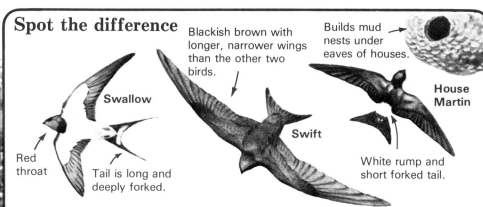

Blackish brown with longer, narrower wings than the other two birds.

Builds mud nests under eaves of houses.

Swallow

House Martin

Red throat

Tail is long and deeply forked.

Swift

White rump and short forked tail.

These birds, which are all summer visitors to Britain, look rather similar. The pictures will help you to identify them. All three catch insects while flying, but they feed at different heights. The Swallow feeds near the ground and is often seen swooping low over water. The House Martin's flight is less swooping and it feeds higher than the Swallow. The Swift feeds much higher in the air than the other two birds.

Spotted Flycatcher

The Spotted Flycatcher, another summer visitor, sits on a tree or post and waits for insects to pass nearby. It flies off to catch its prey, then returns to its perch.

Anting

Mistle Thrush covered with ants.

Some birds rub ants on their feathers or allow ants to crawl over them. They probably do this because a liquid from the ants helps to clean their feathers and rid them of mites.

Roosting

At night, many birds gather together in large numbers for warmth and safety. The tree or building they settle on for the night is called a "roost". Birds may fly many miles each evening to the same roost. In Britain, it is quite common to see thousands of Starlings roosting together.

Life in the water

A garden pond, however small, attracts a variety of wildlife. Many insects will live in or on the water, and frogs and toads may breed there. Birds will come to drink, bathe and hunt for insects, especially if you put a stone for them to settle on.

As more and more farm ponds are being drained, valuable water habitats are lost. Garden ponds can help to replace them. If you make a pond, try to shade part of it with plants and shrubs around the edge to give cover to animals.

Making a pond

Thick layer of newspaper or sand.

Pond should be at least 1m long, 70cm wide and 40cm deep.

It is quite easy to make a small pond in the garden. Start by digging a hole with gently sloping sides. Then make a shallow shelf round the edge for border plants. Smooth the sides and bottom and remove any sharp stones. Place sand or a thick layer of newspaper over the sides and base of the hole.

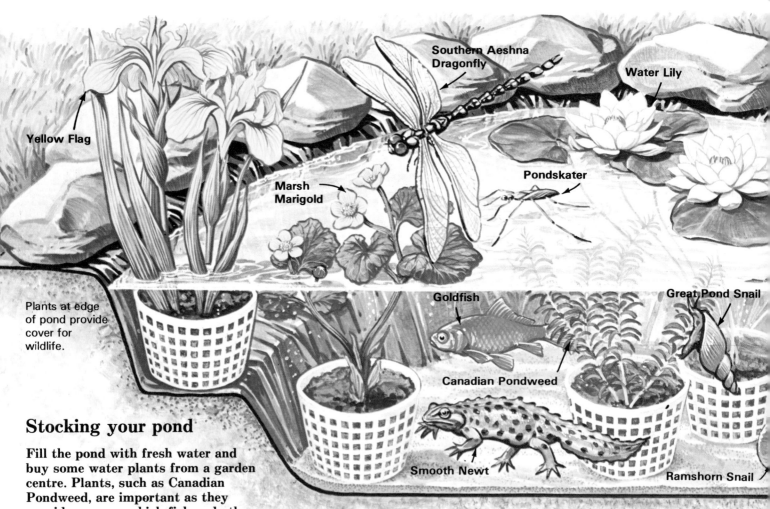

Yellow Flag

Southern Aeshna Dragonfly

Water Lily

Marsh Marigold

Pondskater

Plants at edge of pond provide cover for wildlife.

Goldfish

Great Pond Snail

Canadian Pondweed

Smooth Newt

Ramshorn Snail

Stocking your pond

Fill the pond with fresh water and buy some water plants from a garden centre. Plants, such as Canadian Pondweed, are important as they provide oxygen, which fish and other animals need to breathe. Floating plants, like Water Lilies, provide shade from the sun.

Stock the pond with fish and snails. Other animals, especially insects, will visit the pond to feed and breed.

Some insects, like dragonflies, start life in ponds but leave the water when fully grown. The adults return to water to lay their eggs. Look out for other winged insects hunting for food around the pond.

Frogs, toads and newts spend most of their adult life on land. You may find them hiding in damp corners in your garden. In spring, they go to ponds to mate and lay their jelly-covered eggs or "spawn". Frogspawn is laid in

Life in a tree

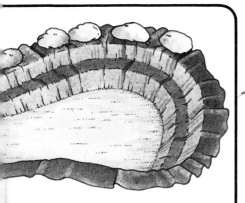

Line the pond with strong polythene, which you can buy at a garden centre. Weight the edge of the plastic down with stones and put sand on the bottom of the pond.

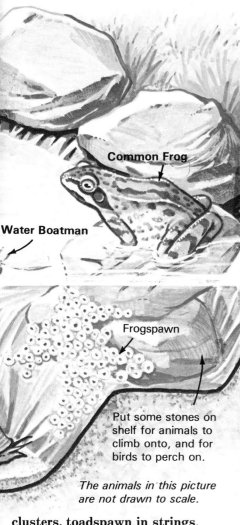

Common Frog

Water Boatman

Frogspawn

Put some stones on shelf for animals to climb onto, and for birds to perch on.

The animals in this picture are not drawn to scale.

clusters, toadspawn in strings. When the young tadpoles hatch, they stay in the water until their lungs and legs develop, then they leave the pond as small adults.

Trees provide food and shelter for a variety of animals. No matter what size or type a tree is, birds and many different kinds of insects and small creatures will use it.

Trees in Britain are either broadleaved, with wide flat leaves, or conifers, with needle-like leaves.

This picture shows you where to look for different types of wildlife on and around trees.

Many birds nest and roost in trees.

Some insect larvae feed inside tree leaves. In reaction the tree forms "galls", like these found on oak leaves. If you cut a gall in half you will find the larva inside.

Squirrels live in trees and are active by day. They feed on tree seeds and nuts. You are more likely to see Grey Squirrels in gardens in Britain, but Red Squirrels are much more common on the Continent.

Climbing plants, like Ivy and Honeysuckle, grow up tree trunks. They provide shelter for animals and do not harm the tree.

If you leave fallen leaves on the ground around trees, insects will hide and feed there. Birds will then come to hunt for the insects.

Toadstools may grow among dead leaves in autumn.

Look for caterpillars on leaves and twigs.

Bracket fungi grow on tree trunks.

Some moths rest on tree trunks during the day. Beetles and other insects live in cracks and behind loose bark.

If you have a fruit tree, leave a few windfalls on the ground to attract butterflies and other insects that feed on the juice of fruit.

The garden at night

Many animals rest during the day and only come out at night. Try exploring your garden at night with a torch covered with red tissue paper. Some animals come out at dusk, others emerge later and are still active at dawn. Go out at these different times and see what you can find.

Some nocturnal animals are quite noisy, so try keeping still and listening carefully for a while. You may hear the grunts of a Hedgehog or the croaking of a Toad.

The flowers of some plants, such as Dandelions, Daisies and the Scarlet Pimpernel, close up at night. Others, like Honeysuckle and Evening Primrose, produce a strong scent at dusk that attracts moths to feed from them.

The **Tawny Owl** is the most common owl in gardens. It hunts at night for mice and other small animals, and may even attack birds while they roost.

The **Hedgehog** is a noisy animal and you may hear it grunting as it hunts for food at night. If you spot one, you can encourage it to return by putting out a saucer of water and some cat or dog food.

The **Green Lacewing** lives on trees and bushes. The larvae and adults feed on aphids.

The **Common Toad** hunts at night for insects and slugs. It always returns to the same place, usually a hole in the ground, to hide during the day.

The male **Dark Bush-cricket** chirps loudly on summer evenings to attract female crickets.

Glow-worms are beetles. On summer nights, the "light" produced by the wingless females attracts the winged males flying above.

The **Wood Mouse** comes out only when it is very dark. It feeds mainly on seeds and berries and will climb bushes to reach fruit.

Ground Beetles hunt for slugs and other small creatures at night.

Bats are active at dusk and just before sunrise. They feed on insects.

Pipistrelle Bat

Long-eared Bat

Foxes hunt at night for small animals and birds. They may visit gardens to scavenge for food in dustbins. They have a strong, musty smell.

Some beetles fly at dusk. They are often attracted to lights and may crash into windows.

Elephant Hawk Moth feeding on **Honeysuckle.**

Heart and Dart Moth on **Evening Primrose.**

The **Common Shrew** needs to eat its own weight in food every day. It spends most of its time hunting for food in hedgerows and long grass and only comes out into the open at night.

Silver-Y Moth on **Night Scented Stock.**

Burnished Brass Moth on **Valerian.**

At night, moths use the moon's light as a guide to flying in straight lines. They do this by keeping the moon's light on the same side of their body. Put a bright light in the garden at night and watch how moths react. As they pass nearby, the moths are confused by the light and try to use it to steer by. Keeping the light on the same side of their body, they fly in a circle, getting closer to the light until finally they fly into it.

27

Visitors to the garden

The different kinds of animals and plants that will visit or live in your garden depend partly on what kind of garden you have (see page 4), and partly on the type of countryside near to it. Here are some of the animals and plants that live in woods, farmland, moors and by the sea, and that may visit, or grow, in gardens near to their natural habitats.

Birds, mammals and insects will visit gardens in their search for food and shelter. Wild plants grow from seeds blown into gardens by the wind. They may also be carried in on the fur of animals, or left behind in the animals' droppings.

Near woodland

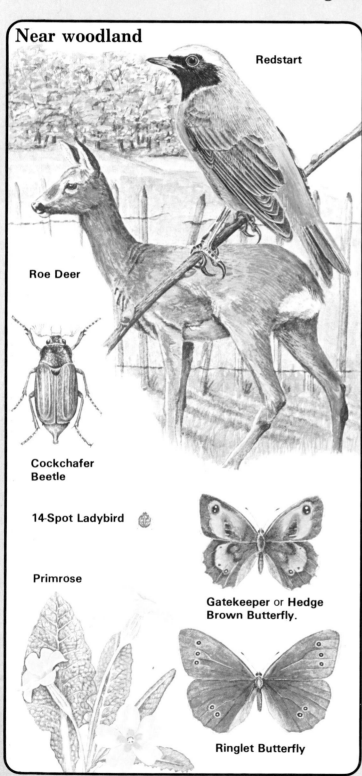

Redstart

Roe Deer

Cockchafer Beetle

14-Spot Ladybird

Primrose

Gatekeeper or Hedge Brown Butterfly.

Ringlet Butterfly

Near the sea

Herring Gulls

Burnet Rose

Yellow Wagtail

Short-winged Conehead (a Bush-cricket)

Sea Pink

Sand Wasp

Near farmland

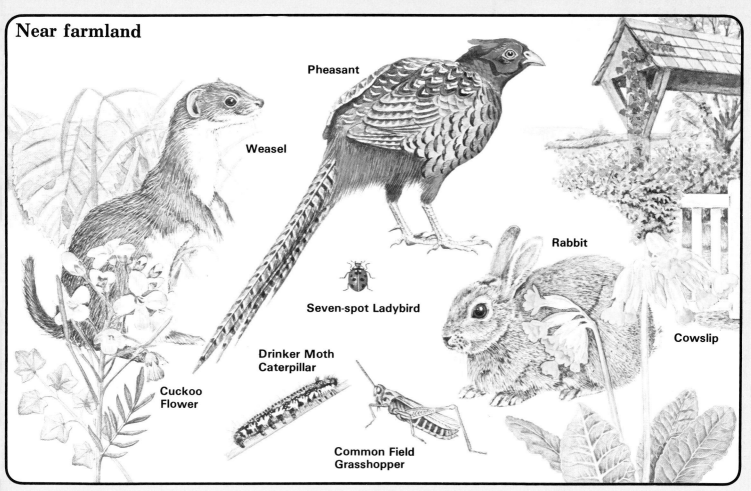

Weasel

Pheasant

Seven-spot Ladybird

Rabbit

Cowslip

Cuckoo Flower

Drinker Moth Caterpillar

Common Field Grasshopper

Near heaths and moors

Oak Eggar Moth

Harebell

Gorse

Adder

Grayling Butterfly

Emperor Moth Caterpillar

Heather

More wildlife in the garden

On flowers and bushes

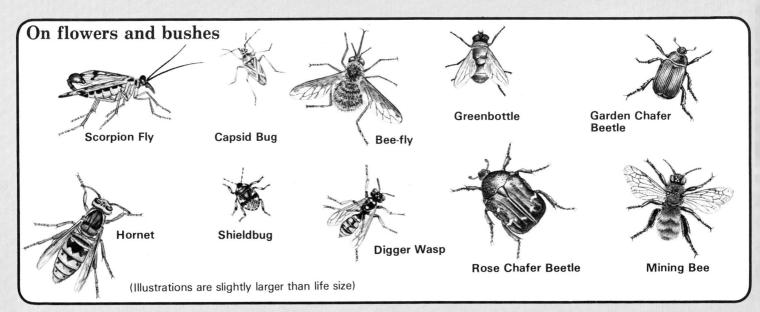

Scorpion Fly

Capsid Bug

Bee-fly

Greenbottle

Garden Chafer Beetle

Hornet

Shieldbug

Digger Wasp

Rose Chafer Beetle

Mining Bee

(Illustrations are slightly larger than life size)

On the ground (The small black shapes show life size)

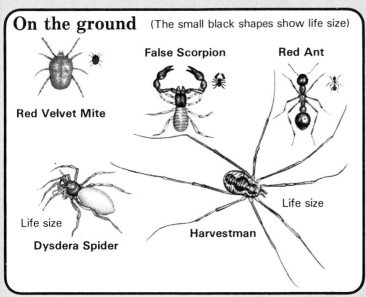

Red Velvet Mite

False Scorpion

Red Ant

Life size

Dysdera Spider

Harvestman

Life size

In the vegetable patch

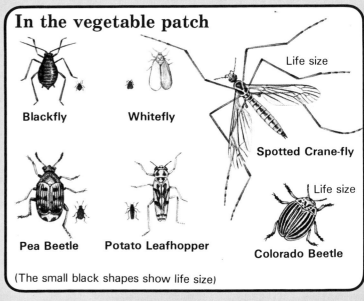

Blackfly

Whitefly

Life size

Spotted Crane-fly

Life size

Pea Beetle

Potato Leafhopper

Colorado Beetle

(The small black shapes show life size)

Caterpillars
(Illustrations are life size)

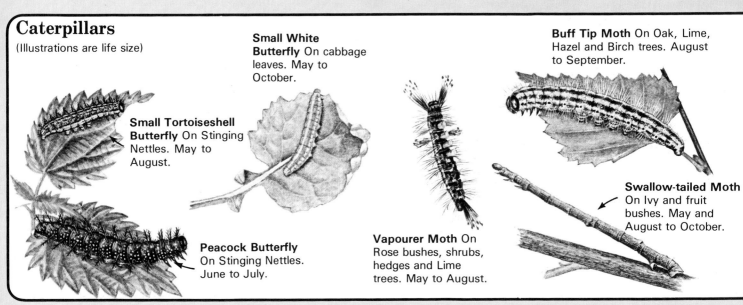

Small White Butterfly On cabbage leaves. May to October.

Buff Tip Moth On Oak, Lime, Hazel and Birch trees. August to September.

Small Tortoiseshell Butterfly On Stinging Nettles. May to August.

Peacock Butterfly On Stinging Nettles. June to July.

Vapourer Moth On Rose bushes, shrubs, hedges and Lime trees. May to August.

Swallow-tailed Moth On Ivy and fruit bushes. May and August to October.

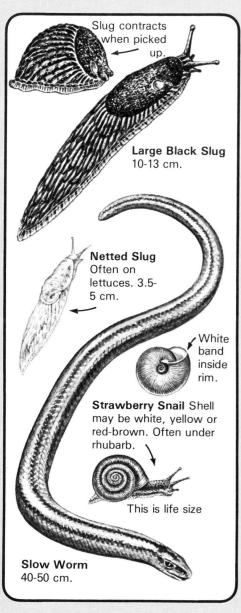

Slug contracts when picked up.

Large Black Slug 10-13 cm.

Netted Slug Often on lettuces. 3.5-5 cm.

White band inside rim.

Strawberry Snail Shell may be white, yellow or red-brown. Often under rhubarb.

This is life size

Slow Worm 40-50 cm.

Magpie Moth On fruit bushes. May to June.

Elephant Hawk Moth On Rosebay Willowherb. July to August.

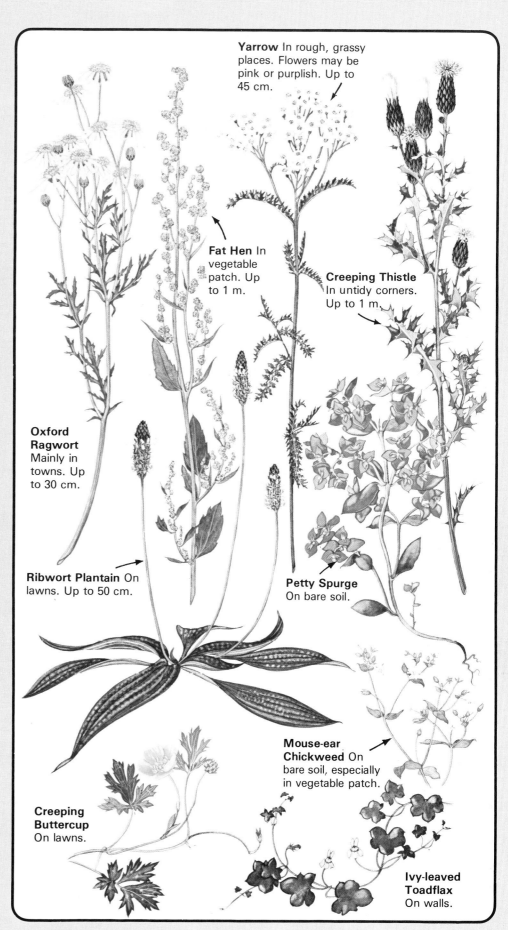

Yarrow In rough, grassy places. Flowers may be pink or purplish. Up to 45 cm.

Fat Hen In vegetable patch. Up to 1 m.

Creeping Thistle In untidy corners. Up to 1 m.

Oxford Ragwort Mainly in towns. Up to 30 cm.

Ribwort Plantain On lawns. Up to 50 cm.

Petty Spurge On bare soil.

Mouse-ear Chickweed On bare soil, especially in vegetable patch.

Creeping Buttercup On lawns.

Ivy-leaved Toadflax On walls.

Index

Books to read

The Natural History of the Garden. Michael Chinery (Collins)
Towns and Gardens. Denis Owen (Hodder & Stoughton)
The Family Naturalist. Michael Chinery (Macdonald and Jane's)
Nature all Around Michael Chinery (Purnell)
Exploring the Garden. Leslie Jackman (Evans)
Nature Day and Night. Richard Adams (Kestrel)
The Insects in your Garden. Harold Oldroyd (Kestrel)
Hedgehogs, Spiders, Bees and Wasps, and other titles. Young Naturalist Books (Priory Press)

Wild Life begins at home. Tony Soper (Pan)
Oasis is a magazine about conservation gardening. It is published quarterly and is available by post. If you are interested, write to "Oasis", P.O. Box 237, London SE13 5QU

Clubs and societies

The Council for Environmental Conservation (address: Zoological Gardens, Regents Park, London NW1 4RY) will supply the addresses of your local **Natural History Societies.** (Send a stamped, addressed envelope for a free list.) Many of these have wild flower sections and almost all have field meetings. **The Royal Society for Nature Conservation** (address: 22, The Green, Nettleham, Lincoln) will give you the address of your **County Naturalist Trust,** which may have a junior branch. Many of the Trusts have meetings, lectures, and opportunities for work on reserves.

The **Watch Club** is a club for 8 to 15 year-olds who are interested in nature and the environment. For a small annual subscription members are sent a copy of the magazine **Watchword** three times a year. The magazine contains details of surveys and other projects and activities for members to join in from home. Write to Watch, 22 The Green, Nettleham, Lincoln LN2 2NR